60 WAYS TO RELIEVE ~~STRESS~~ IN 60 SECONDS

60 WAYS TO RELIEVE STRESS IN 60 SECONDS

By Manning Rubin
Illustrated by Paul Frahm

WORKMAN PUBLISHING, NEW YORK

To Jane,
who has always given me
constructive stress.

Copyright © 1993 by Manning Rubin

All rights reserved. No portion of this book may be reproduced—
mechanically, electronically, or by any other means, including
photocopying—without written permission of the publisher. Published
simultaneously in Canada by Thomas Allen & Son, Ltd.

Library of Congress Cataloging-in-Publication Data

Rubin, Manning.
    60 ways to relieve stress in 60 seconds / by Manning Rubin;
illustrated by Paul Frahm.
        p.   cm.
    ISBN 1-56305-338-1 (pbk.) $5.95
    1. Stress management.   I. Title.   II. Title: Sixty ways to reduce
stress in sixty seconds.
RA785.R8   1993   92-50932
155.9′042—dc20   CIP

Workman books are available at special discounts when purchased in
bulk for premiums and special sales promotions as well as for fund-
raising or educational use. Special editions or book excerpts can also
be created to specification. For details, contact the Special Sales
Director at the address below.

Workman Publishing
708 Broadway
New York, NY 10003

First printing May 1993

10 9 8 7 6 5 4 3 2 1

FOREWORD

A *Time* magazine cover story labeled stress "The Epidemic of the Eighties," and numerous surveys since then reveal that the problem has steadily escalated. Why all the sudden fuss? After all, stress has been around since Adam and Eve met in the Garden of Eden. A major reason is that contemporary stresses are more pervasive, pernicious and persistent than those experienced by prior generations. Job stress is a major factor and has been described by some authorities as America's leading adult health problem. Another reason for the heightened interest in stress is that we know much more about how it contributes to heart attacks, colds, cancer, ulcers, AIDS, low back pain, and other "diseases of civilization."

A variety of stress reduction strategies are available, including meditation, yoga, jogging, muscular relaxation exercises, visual imagery, biofeedback, and the like. However, just as stress is different for each one of us, no single stress-reduction approach works for everybody. For certain individuals, some might actually prove stressful. In addition, many can't find the time or funds required to master some of these techniques, much less practice them on a regular basis.

All too often stress is due not to external events, but rather to our perception of them. Many of us can benefit greatly by learning to put things in perspective, and finding some way temporarily to escape from the daily grind may help in this regard. The following pages contain a number of simple but useful exercises that you can practice in various settings to give you that kind of breather, whenever you need it. Think of them as little, free oases in the desert of daily stress, and find the ones that work best for you.

"Don't sweat the small stuff"—and remember that most of the time it's *all* small stuff. This little volume can facilitate your appreciation of that and also help you learn how to take time to smell the roses.

Paul J. Rosch, M.D., F.A.C.P., President, The American Institute of Stress
Clinical Professor of Medicine and Psychiatry, New York Medical College

*E*very day brings more and more information about stress. Because of stress on the job, millions of dollars are wasted on lower productivity, increased medical costs and absenteeism. And what stress does to personal and family relationships is documented chaos. Burnout, breakups, breakdowns, poor performance—all can be traced to stress.

What this book offers is a simple, day-to-day strategy for reducing and controlling the effects of stress. Conceived along the lines of cognitive therapy, a school of psychiatry that teaches you how to comfort yourself, it draws on the most popular sources of solace such as eating, listening to music or watching television, and recalling happy memories. By consciously distracting yourself, you can exercise control over your emotions and feelings. And the more you do these mental calisthenics, the easier it becomes to take charge.

But, you ask, is 60 seconds really long enough to relieve stress? Try waiting a full minute after you ask someone to pass the cream for your coffee, especially if it's the first cup of the day. Or count slowly all the way to 60 and see how much time goes by.

The truth is, a minute is a long time—certainly long enough to calm yourself down if you use it properly. Of course, this technique won't eliminate the *source* of your stress, but it will help you handle the symptoms when they occur. The trick is to act promptly. Don't let your stressful feelings magnify: when the adrenaline starts pumping or the breath starts shortening, when the anger or frustration builds or the disappointment deepens, learn to recognize it. Make up your mind to interrupt what you're doing and put one of the 60 exercises to work. You can pick any one at any time, and you can add your own variations. And when you finish, make it a point to remind yourself that you've just exercised mind control.

Once you feel comfortable with this do-it-yourself power, you'll begin to recognize stress building up before it gets too far and you'll find that defusing it can become second nature. And maybe that's when you can start figuring out why it happens in the first place.

*C*rumple a
piece of paper
into a ball and play
"basketball" using
your wastebasket
or other receptacle.

*C*hoose a favorite fantasy and carry it out in your mind.

*W*alk around the office while remembering in detail all the ingredients of one of your favorite meals.

*G*et up and look out the window. Study something out there so you can describe it in detail after 1 minute.

*M*ake yourself laugh out loud. Think of something funny to get yourself started.

*S*tand up and do some stretching exercises.

*G*et up from your chair and straighten up your desk or work area as quickly as you can.

*C*lose your eyes
and let your
mind go blank.

*G*uess how many steps it will take to walk to a spot nearby— the water fountain, coffee machine, bathroom or front door. Then walk there and see how close you came.

*T*ry to recall the contents of your pockets, briefcase or handbag. Write down as many items as you can.

*C*all the weather or some other information service. Try to memorize exactly what they say.

*C*lose your eyes and think of a color; then picture 5 things of that color.

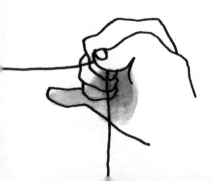

*W*alk to and from the bathroom twice before you use it, observing everything you pass along the way.

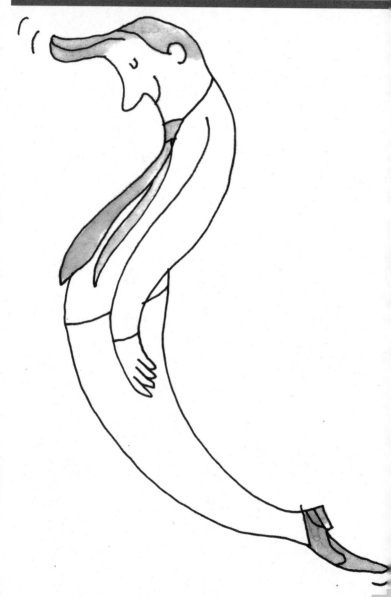

*C*lose your
eyes and
make yourself
"feel" a wave of
relaxation that
starts at your head
and goes down
to your toes.

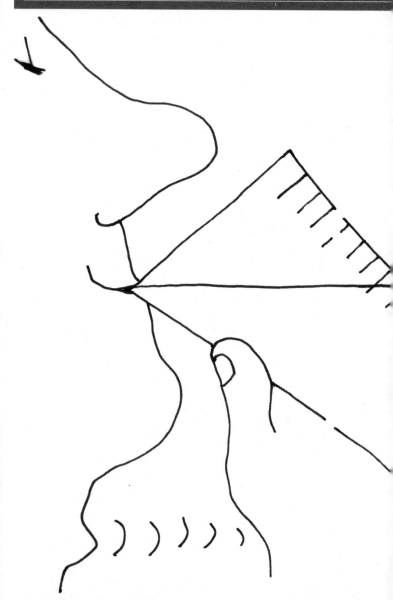

***D*rink a glass of water in exactly 30 sips.**

*N*ame as
many U.S.
presidents as you
can in 1 minute.*

*How about vice presidents?

*C*lose your eyes and hum "Twinkle, Twinkle, Little Star." Other tunes to try: "The Star-Spangled Banner," "America the Beautiful," the first song you referred to as "our song."

*M*unch on a candy bar, snack or piece of fruit in small bites that you take precisely every 10 seconds.

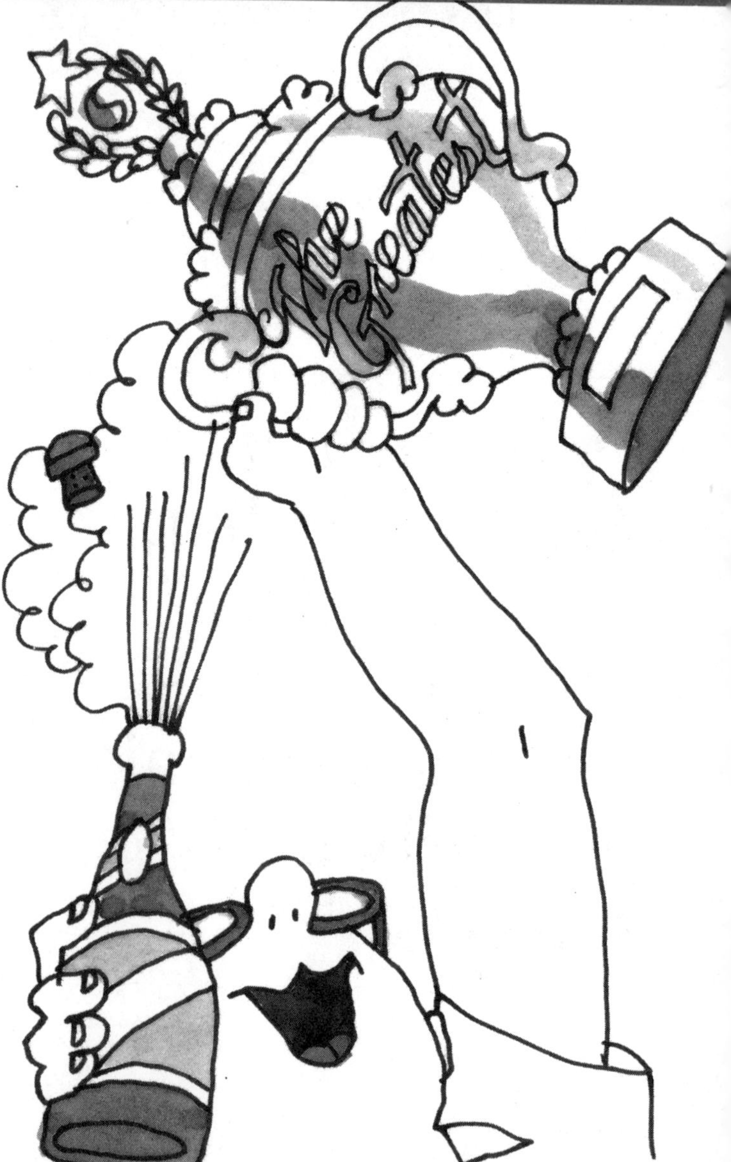
The Greatest!

*C*lose your
eyes and
visualize
your greatest
achievement.

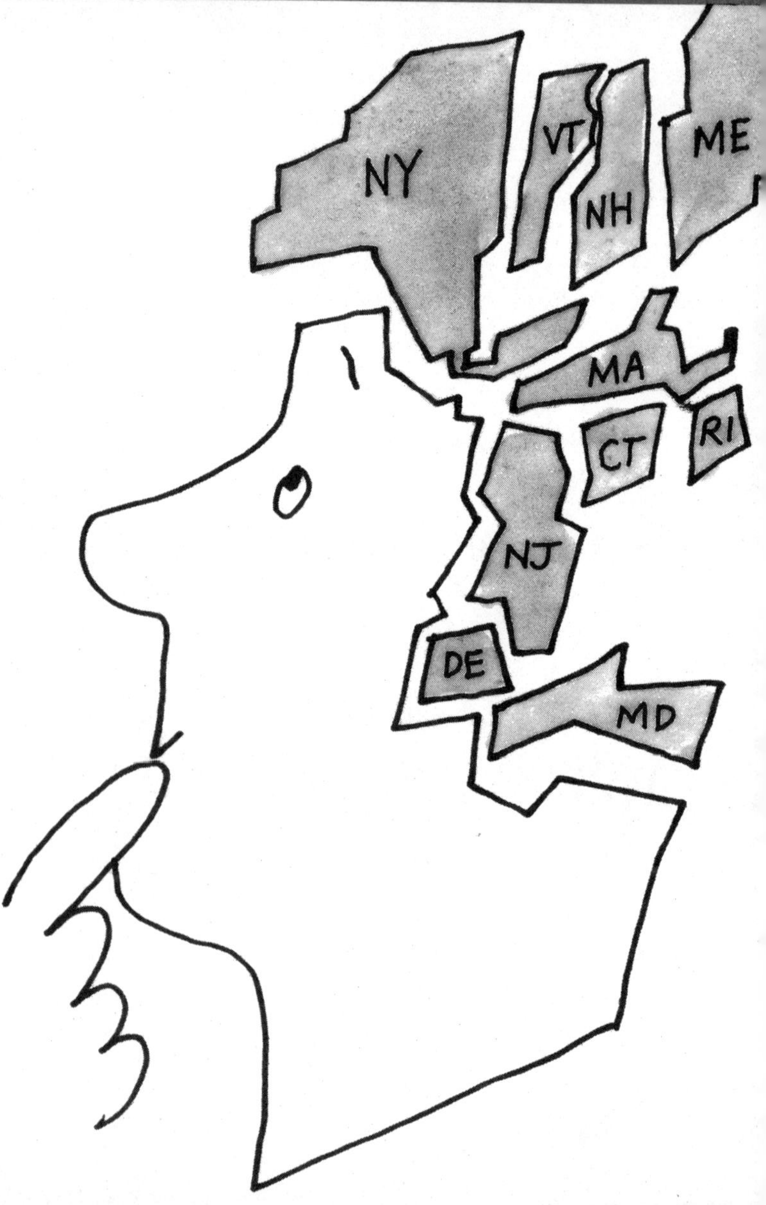
NY
VT
NH
ME
MA
RI
CT
NJ
DE
MD

*W*rite down the names of all 50 states—or as many as you can in 1 minute.*

*How about state capitals?

*S*tand on
tiptoe as long
as you can.

7

*S*ee if you can point your finger or a pencil at something for 60 seconds without shaking.

*C*lose your eyes and picture ocean waves breaking on a beach. Try to "hear" them.*

*Or how about imagining a beautiful sunset over a lake?

*C*lose your eyes
and take slow,
deep breaths.
Visualize the air
coming in and
going out.*

*Or see how long you can
hold your breath.

*T*ry to stand several coins—pennies, nickels, dimes or quarters —on edge.

*D*o isometric exercises by pushing one part of your body against another.

*S*tare at your work area. Close your eyes and reach for— or walk over to— something you saw without touching anything else.

*S*tare at an object for 60 seconds without blinking, then close your eyes and "see" it.

*S*uck on a hard candy and think *only* of its flavor.

*P*retend you're holding up a wall and imagine it falling if you let go. What would happen?

*M*ake a list of 5 great movies, books, inventions or the like.

*P*retend you're a reporter covering a story—any story. Describe it to yourself as a TV newsperson would.

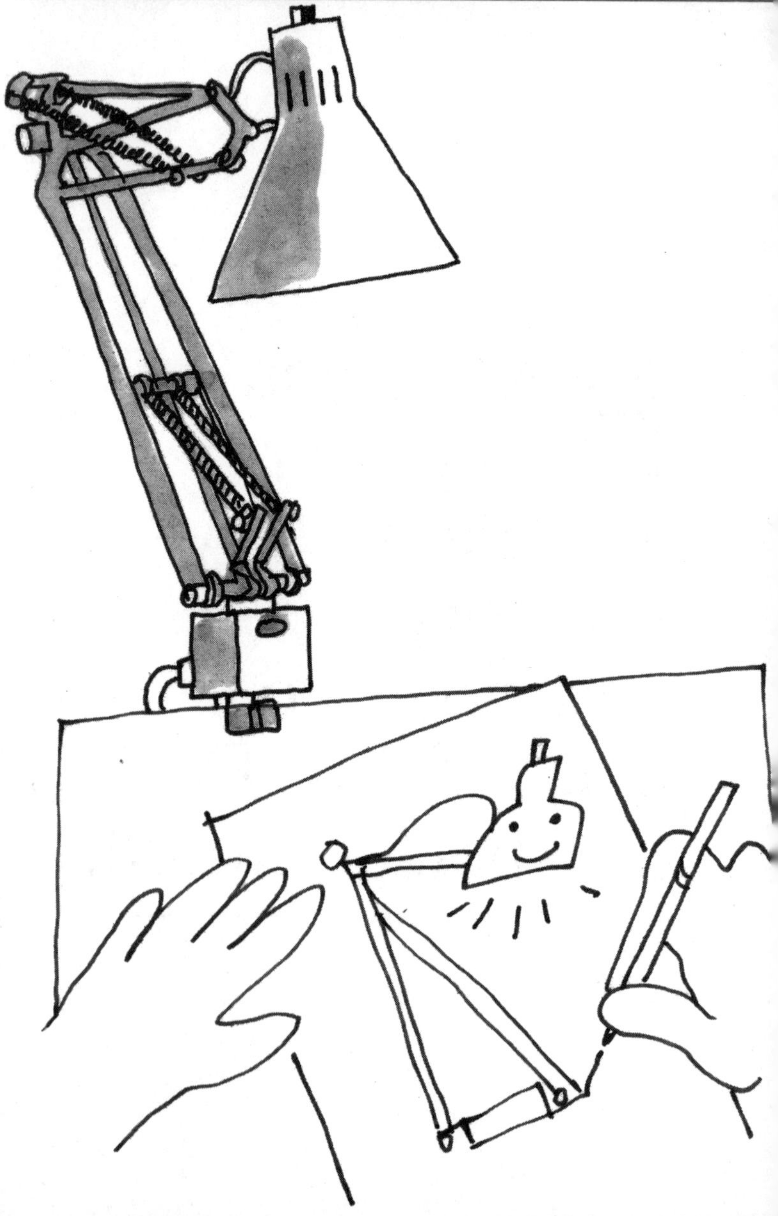

*T*ry to draw
  a nearby
object—a chair,
a plant, your
computer.

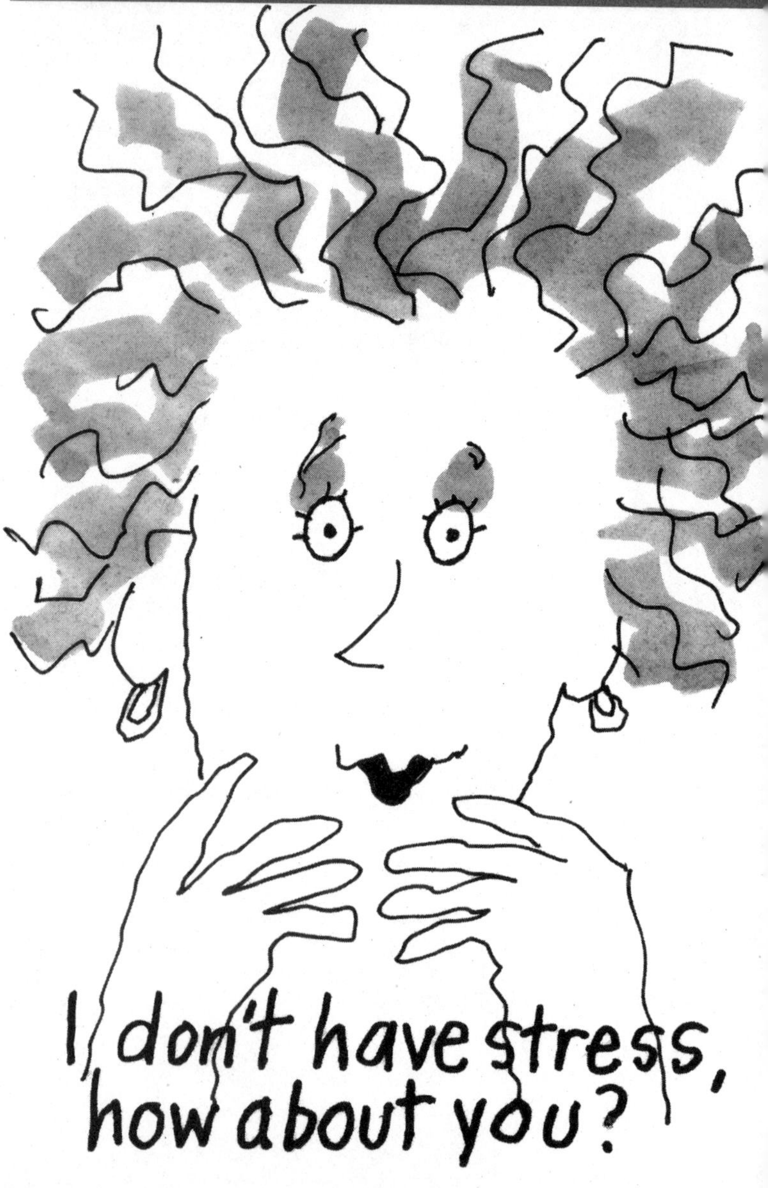
I don't have stress,
how about you?

*M*ake up your own ending to "roses are red, violets are blue . . ."

*P*ick an age between 5 and 15 or 15 and 25. Try to remember where you lived at that age and who your friends were, etc.

*N*ame as many professional teams as you can in a specific sport.

*C*ount
backwards
from 100 or say
the alphabet
backwards as fast
as you can.

*P*ick a word like "I," "you," "the," "baby," "she" or "he," and think of 5 song titles or lyrics that begin with that word.

*L*ist as many
4-legged
animals* as you
can (or draw
them).

*Or fish or flying animals.

*C*lose your eyes and visualize being cuddled, caressed and soothed by someone you desire.

*I*magine a scene where you enter and save the day by standing up to someone.

*L*ist 10 things you've most enjoyed in the past week, month or year, or in your life. (Keep the list.)

*P*icture yourself starring in a movie. Who would your co-star be?

*I*magine that you inherited 10 million dollars. What's the first thing you would do with the money? What else would you do?

*S*pend a minute thinking about a completely new job or career. What would you choose?

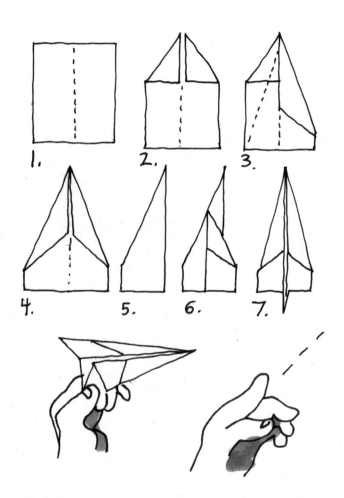

*M*ake a paper airplane and sail it across the room.

*W*ithout using your thumb at all, pick up a pencil or pen with the hand you don't normally use. Write your name.

*C*lose your
eyes and try
to draw a perfect
circle.

*L*isten to the sound of something nearby—the air conditioner, traffic, or such. Close your eyes and turn it into a soothing sound.

*S*top what you're doing. Listen to the radio for 1 minute. Concentrate so you can repeat what you heard.

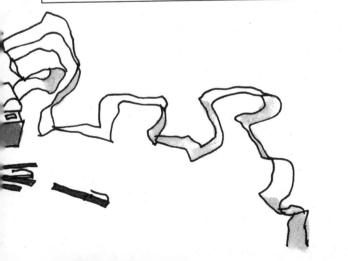

*T*ake off your shoes and wiggle your toes freely; then put your shoes back on.

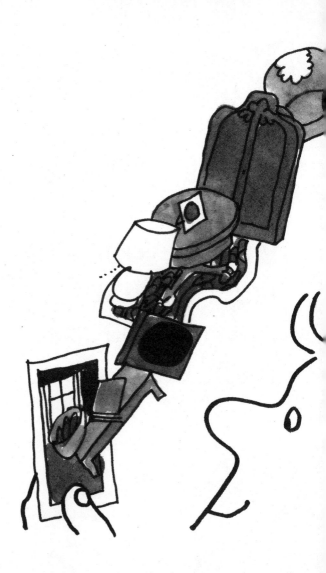

*P*icture another room in your home and write down its contents from memory.

*C*omb your hair in a completely different style.

*C*lose your
   eyes and
visualize a warm,
happy moment in
your life.

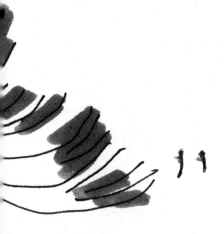

*D*o 10 jumping jacks, push-ups, knee bends or sit-ups.

*G*ive your pet
a 60-second
scratch.

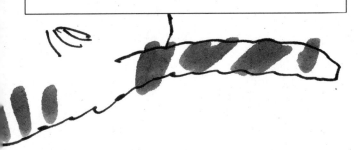

*I*nstantly stop what you're doing and change position, using very slow and exaggerated movements as if you were a robot.

***B*alance something on top of your head.**

*L*ie down, cover your head with your arms and let your dog try to lick your face.

9 10

*L*ist 10 things you'd like to do this week, this month, this year or in your lifetime. (Keep the list.)